UShip

What you need to know

T.R. Lewis

DEDICATION

One would have no other choice other than dedicating to the morons that choose to ship and or become a transporter for UShip.

Bless your little heart

Contents

ACKNOWLEDGMENTS

My story of how to and not to not only ship but also how to be a transporter with UShip. I started out and tried to use them exclusively and yes that was a huge mistake. Read this book to the end and you will not make the same stupid ass mistakes that I have made. The information in this book is entirely from my experience and can save you a lot of heartaches and money.

It's plain to see from my book that I hate illegal shippers and I hate them for multiple reasons. Besides the fact that they are the scum of the earth they are the lowest form of a transporter out there and cause nothing but a bad name and lower prices to those of us that work our asses off to do things the correct way.

If your stupid enough to become a transporter or to ship with UShip then good luck to you and this book is a must read.

This book should be read by anyone wishing to ship their property with UShip or become a transporter, however it should be noted that I am in no way affiliated with UShip and the UShip name, trademark and other items belongs to UShip and is only used here to reflect my opinion and experiences with the company through over 130,000 miles of transporting shit across the United States.

Shipping with UShip

Ok so you want to ship with UShip Let's start by saying you're a special kind of stupid, bless your little heart.

Ok well to get started there are a lot of things in the shipping world you need to know however the very first things you need to do is figure out how much do you value your property? How important is the lowest shipping price? If you don't value your property then thanks for buying this book but you don't need it feel free to get any person you run into to transport your crap.

Assuming you place some value on your property then one very important factor to know is there are different kinds of transporters out there, the illegal kind and the legal kind.

The illegal transporter under bids everyone else and provides a service at pennies on the mile.

The legal transporter however has overhead and usually is $1.00 and up per mile.

"What's the difference as long as I get a good price?" you say. Then I say you're a moron!! And again you don't need this book. However I have a chapter to detailed description of both legal and illegal and encourage you to check them and read completely. Go ahead I'll wait for you.

Ok now you are armed with a bit of knowledge and should be a bit better off than before. Feel free to pass along then differences to your friends as you would be surprised how many idiots haven't got a clue.

Things that you need to look out for when choosing a transporter with UShip are;

1) Look on their profile for the SW (Safer watch) badge. This means they are legal. If they don't have it **don't use them.**
2) Another big thing on their profile that sticks out like a sore thumb is a profile that states they will "treat your property like theirs".
   a. This is bad for multiple reasons and here just one example.

Joe the transporter picks up your brand new custom made off road motorcycle.

Joe gives you a great price however Joe needs to make enough money to pay bills so he also books a horse trailer going about the same place (He has to after all because the morons that's using UShip don't want to pay a fair price.)

Joe picks up the motorcycle from you and then heads on over to grab the horse trailer. Now this horse trailer is a 3 horse trailer so Joe kind of won the lottery here, you see he's going to put your motorcycle in one stall and look for a couple of horses heading the same way. One of many problems with this is that a horse trailer isn't made to haul motorcycles so it has to be strapped in anyway Joe can get it.

Now Joe after spending two to three days getting completely loaded decides he needs a quick break so he swings by his home. Shouldn't be an issue after all he's worked hard so far.

Joe decides that he's earned himself a test run on your custom motorcycle (come on moron he said he would treat it like his) so he spends a few hours riding it and then places it back in the trailer, all is fine. Well mostly it would be however now the new bike is dripping a bit of oil and gas into the horse trailer.

The next day Joe continues on and delivers the horses and the trailer to their proper places. Unfortunately the horses are a bit off, most likely from the fumes but its all good they will recover and the owner of the horses as well as the trailer are none the wiser.

Joe then delivers you're not so new motorcycle to you and you notice that it has scuffs on it from straps in places it shouldn't. You also notice that the bike isn't as clean as it should be (Joe did wash the mud off) so you look at the hour gauge and see that it went from zero hours to ten hours. As you continue checking it out you see that this new motorcycle has a scratched fender.

You get mad and start telling the transporter about this and demand he makes all right again. However he laughs at you and says that's how I got it goodbye.

Now you're left with no recourse because you didn't do your homework. You think well I'll turn a claim into his insurance company but then you remember you're a moron and he's not legal and doesn't have an insurance company.

"Wait everyone has insurance right?" Again you're a moron!! No there are two kinds of insurance and if you expect an illegal transporter to have commercial insurance you're a special kind of stupid. If you expect an illegal transporters regular insurance to cover it well here's some news for you. All insurance have long contracts and buried within them are clauses, one clause in particular will state that during illegal activities there is no recourse (I shortened it). So now the DOT requires a transporter to have DOT and MC numbers and to have them you have to have commercial insurance. If you don't have them and you conduct highway commerce then you are breaking the law.

The point that I am making here is your shit out of

luck and have no recourse. You hired someone to conduct an illegal activity and that I. Its self makes you an accomplice as well (ignorance of the law is no excuse). You could sue however that's like a drug addict suing because his dope isn't good. You broke the law and want the law to help you because it didn't work out your way. You should be happy the transporter didn't wreck and kill someone, because you as an accomplice could be liable as well and loose everything you own over the piece of crap that you wanted to ship at pennies on the dollar.

What's that you say? "You hired a legal transporter" great then file a complaint with the DOT as well as with UShip and his insurance company to be compensated. Wow that was easy, now wasn't it? Not much of a hassle at all when you do things the correct way.

3) Reviews are a good thing to look at however unless they are legal there are no amount of positive reviews that can justify me using an illegal shipper.
4) Photos are good too as long as the equipment in the photographs is the same thing that shows up to your house.
5) Profiles that have descriptions are also good however watch out for those that think you should hire them based on their past professions.

Ok Let's Start

Now you should be mainly ready to ship at least you know who to look out for at this point. Now let's look at what to expect and how to get a good price.

You've probably have looked at UShip's estimator and think that you can get those rates, again you're a special kind of stupid if you believe that crap. Here is the problem with the estimator that they have online. First it is based on prices that they have had for similar items and routes and if your remember correctly most of their shippers are illegal and if you don't remember then you need to get someone else to read this to you, this book isn't that long. Take those numbers and that experience and throw it out the window and mark it off as a waste of your time, time you could of spent with a loved one but you will never be able to regain it.

As a basic rule if you get a rate of $1.00 per mile you're doing good right? Wrong moron "Why I thought you said a buck a mile for legal shippers" you say? Well the problem there is you forgot that UShip is taking a large portion of that, the amount will vary depending on what it is your shipping. I would consider 25% of the fee is going to UShip and they will dispute this but based on my own numbers of the many loads I have carried for them that would be a good average. Now you say "Why don't the transporters just say $1.00 per mile plus fees" and that's a good question however UShip does not permit the transporters to EVER mention the fees to the shipper. When I tried I got flagged and blocked, deleting all of my bids and marking my account as suspended. "What do they have to say about that" you say? Well they told me that any mention of a fee would confuse the shipper and they want a pleasant experience for the shipper. Now I can't print the fee terms here because they would complain but check them out, act like you want to be a transporter and accept a bid, you will be surprised. I said to them "So you don't want they shipper to be confused but from your fee terms it would take a rocket scientist to figure out the fees?" they didn't like that and of course blocked me again.

Ok so you've got a price to base a good choice on accepting a bid, $1.25 per mile. So now what?

Place your add

Ok now you've placed your add and you are waiting for a good price to come through. You've got plenty of illegal shippers bidding and willing to transport your $25,000.00 boat 2,000 miles for $500.00 but be patient and ignore them they are like cockroaches.

You will notice that there are some that have a reasonable rate and some that have really high rates that are legal. The thing to remember you have time to wait.

You might see a rate that is lower then what we determined was a good rate and it is from a legal shipper. That's good because he probably needs what is called a back haul (He needs to get to another location without paying for expenses himself and losing money). I generally stay away from these unless they have an expiration on the bid. If they have an expiration on the bid then they generally need a backhaul and have a load on the other end that needs picked up at a certain time. If they don't have an expiration then they are just playing with you and aren't the kind of shippers that you really want to use anyways.

A word of advice that's worth noting is that most truck drivers drive for a reason, they are generally not real good with people and are either real passive or in most cases dicks. This doesn't have to bother you because they can usually put on a different hat for a short time to negotiate good terms and then get the hell out of there.

You always want to make sure that you get a copy of the insurance binder and call the insurance company to verify that it is still good.

I personally would find the company that was legal and had the best price and reviews and at that point I would go to

http://safer.fmcsa.dot.gov/CompanySnapshot.aspx

Look up their name and under the MC number get their telephone number. "Why" you say again like a moron? Well its simple if you call that number up then you can take a $1.25 a mile bid that he is only getting $1.00 out of it after UShip takes their fees and tell him you will pay him $1.10 per mile. He makes more money, you pay less and you both are happier for the experience.

Now Ship

Ok so now you've got your shipper and you have your price, great you're ready to go. Remember you always want to make sure that you get a copy of the insurance binder and call the insurance company to verify that it is still good.

You also want to make sure you get the cell phone number of the driver along with the estimated date of arrival. You should make the driver call you at least once a day to give you updates and that usually keeps the driver motivated and moving even if he gripes a bit about it.

Make sure you have pictures of your shipment before and after delivery in case there are any issues, this can only help.

Never pay advances and never let the driver call you and talk you into sending money to them. There are circumstances where you may have to pay out of pocket expenses on the road such as your equipment (Not his) broke down and needs repaired to continue to haul. In those cases pay the company that is doing the repairs not the driver.

If you were still a moron and used UShip to ship

then make sure you follow up with a review for the driver as this is his lively hood and it will help other shippers identify a good or bad driver.

Being a Transporter

There are lots of reasons why one might want to become a transporter and some legitimate reasons. The most popular one is that you want to own your own profitable business. While owning a business is one thing owning a profitable business is an entirely other thing. There are many factors in becoming a profitable business that one has to take into consideration and this book just refers to the basics and how UShip can screw that up.

In this section we will go over the issues of using UShip as a transporter.

Basics

Ok so you want to be a transporter and use UShip, your just plain ole stupid and there is little help for you however I will offer what knowledge I was able to obtain from my experience as a legal shipper that yes unfortunately used UShip.

Yes that's correct I did use UShip when I first started out however I quickly learned that with their bent sense of fairness and their willingness to protect the illegal shippers that I needed to change my business model and fast.

If you decide to use UShip exclusively you will go out of business, you will lose there is no model in which you can come out ahead that way and you cannot be helped. UShip caters to those who make them money.

"Who makes UShip money" you say? That's simple, those who win the bids and those are going to be illegal transporters 98% of the time. So you will notice that you cannot degrade an illegal transporter in any way or UShip will block you. This includes in your profile, comments and bids you are not permitted to warn shippers of the illegal activities that UShip promotes and harvest and cherishes.

"How can I make money then" again you ask before I get there? That is complicated but not entirely impossible if you follow a few basic rules. One important rule is not to ever take UShip serious and to never rely on UShip.

Only use UShip when it becomes absolutely necessary to do so for a back haul else you're just wasting you money and time.

Now just because I am me I have included sections to explain the differences between illegal and legal shippers and I suggest you read them, if you become one of the dickheads that ships illegally then you aren't worth my time and shouldn't have bought this book to start with.

Always remember that pricing doesn't only affect you but the entire industry so NEVER underprice your services, you aren't doing anyone any favors and that load isn't worth hurting your entire year's income over.

Never haul other loads inside or on a shipper's trailer that's just ghetto and illegal and can and will come around and eventually bite you in the ass. Remember we are legal shippers.

Answer your telephone every time it rings, if you're a lazy ass then you won't make it and if your hiding from someone then change your number but when building a business shippers like to be able to get you the first time every time they call and not a recording.

Build Your Client List

That's right sounds simple doesn't, well pay attention moron and you might learn a thing or two.

When browsing for loads on UShip pay attention to a few key things;

1) Loads that ship from the same location.
2) Loads that always deliver to the same location.
3) Loads that you can handle.

Those two things are the single most important items that UShip has to offer and will take you a long way. Don't bid on those loads because if you win the bid you will have to haul them and give UShip 25% of your hard earned money.

Note the name of the person that posted the loads then go to google and google the city and the type of company that would be shipping from or to the locations that are noted. I will use RV companies as an example.

Make a list and start calling the RV companies and asking for the person listed on the UShip bid, when you get the right company then you have just made a contact that if your IQ is above any ass wipe then you should be able to get the load. Example;

Hey this is John Smith and I notice you have a load going to Miami and I would like to introduce myself to you. (Give him a second to respond and if it's positive) I own a legal insured transportation company and I would love to give you a great rate on that load.

Then simply give him a rate and see if he wants to negotiate or accept it. If he says I only go through UShip then simply apologize for his stupidity and say thank you for your time then move on because he isn't worth hauling for.

Remember there are tons of shippers out there that post with no intent of ever accepting a bid but only with the intention of letting you know they have a load that needs transported.

Also don't be afraid of asking around for new contacts, a lot of legal shippers don't mind helping out other legal shippers. I once had a RV dealer send me across the street to his competitor to haul loads for him as well.

Always be sure to introduce yourself to other legal shippers you see on the road. A lot of times they have advice as well as extra loads and they can also help you when you over book or have a breakdown. This is a resource that one cannot put a value on so keep saying hello.

When you're forced to walk with the Snakes

There are times that you will use UShip for back hauls or whatever may be the reason, the key here is to keep it to a minimal and make the best out of a bad situation. Just remember who they are and tread lightly with them. Some claim you can make a living using just them however I have learned it is just the illegal transporters that make that claim.

Always work to build your client list that doesn't rely on UShip. You can do this by having business cards that you hand to the shipper when you meet as well as talking to the shipper and have them refer you to their family and friends. That will go a long way towards getting a new independent client. Also always let the shipper know of the fees that UShip charges and that if they call you direct they can get a price break.

Never bid to low that just hurts you and other legal transporters. If the shipper wants things shipped for pennies on the dollar let the illegal asshole put their property in the ditch somewhere because they deserve each other. Bidding low is worse than being a scab at a union strike.

Make sure that under your terms in the bid you clearly state that the shipper not you is responsible for all repairs that may be needed as well as the shipper must make sure that their unit is road worthy if it's a trailer.

Always check tires and trailer out to make sure it is road worthy never take the client's word for it they will lie if they think it will save them money, remember they are looking for the cheapest transporter not the best so be patient with the morons but be firm. In the end you are responsible for the safety of the shipment.

Never ever take a load you're not comfortable hauling, you can kill someone and that gut feeling is saying "hey stupid don't do it" so listen to it. I can't tell you how many times I've seen transporters all twisted up alongside the road holding up traffic as the paramedics scrape them off the pavement. This always pisses me off because it slows me down and gives us all a bad name.

When talking to the fine people at UShip

Remember fundamental rules of the industry. They are idiots and complete morons trained in only making UShip money and couldn't care less about you especially if you're a legal shipper. Here is a guideline to follow.

1) Talk to them like they are five year old's.
   a. Remember they are stupid.
2) Be polite, always be polite.
   a. Like most morons they have power and they have no ideal on how to handle it.
   b. If you offend them they will block you.
   c. They love to act like they know everything.
3) They will send an email documenting the call most of the time.
   a. Careful what you say.
4) They will every time side with the illegal shippers.
   a. Don't bother complaining about the illegal shipper that way under bid you.

       b. Don't worry about what the illegal
          shipper says in a comment.

5) If you get blocked or suspended and call
    because of it.

       a. Be polite.

       b. Act stupid, remember they are power
          hungry so the more you let them
          think they have the more they will
          act in your favor.

       c. Apologize even know it's their stupid
          policies that caused the suspension.

Those rules will go a long way to ensuring you're happy or as happy as one can be while being screwed like a two dollar whore. If you still have problems then you apparently haven't read this and need to either start over or give it up.

Always remember it is the illegal shippers that makes UShip the bulk of their money so they will always side with the money makers. Tread lightly and follow this books guidelines. There is nothing you can do about it except accept it and move on, you can't change them you can only adapt to the best of the worse situation for a legal transporter.

Create Saved Searches

Now that you have a couple of clients lined up you can actually use UShip for something productive. Create a search either from the city your client ships from or to the city you client ships to. Save this search with the option that it emails you when there are new shipments available. This means that if Supreme RV posts a new load then you automatically get a notification from it instantly.

You will want as many of these as you have clients and you want to make sure that you use these. The more you have the more loads you can end up with.

Some rules for creating a search;

1) You can't have too many of them.
2) Use the filters.
    a. By selecting the type of freight that you want to haul you eliminate the bull shit from the results.
3) Figure out the routes you want to travel.
    a. Some people like me do not go to states that are dickheads and do not permit you to protect yourself. So if you're like me and carry a firearm

everywhere you go then you need to make sure you don't haul into those states.

b. It's nice to know that you're traveling the same highways. Because you get regular stops at restaurants and get to know where you can get something repaired if you're in a familiar area.

4) Make sure your search is for loads that you and your equipment are capable of hauling,

5) Again, you can't have too many saved searches.

If you follow these rules then you're sure to have load possibilities that can help you on cutting down your deadheading. As always I will advise to only use UShip as a last result and DO NOT RELY on UShip or you will fail as a transporter.

Illegal Shipper

Ok you've made it to the page that explains what an illegal shipper is, it's not an illegal Mexican however I've seen them as well transporting with UShip. An illegal shipper is simply someone who decides that the rules don't apply to them and they can make lots more money by not following the laws that are out there.

A quick note is that it would appear that UShip has no problems with illegal shippers and in my experience they actually do everything possible to protect them and keep you from knowing or being told that they are illegal. A quick example is that if a transporter makes a remark that the other bidders are illegal then UShip will immediately flag your transporter account and delete the post. When a transporter calls UShip and notifies them that there is an illegal transporter then UShip will claim that they have no way to prove that.

Illegal transporters usually have poor equipment, little to no experience and defiantly no commercial insurance, no DOT number, no MC number.

Its law that all persons doing intrastate transportation for hire have DOT number and MC numbers. These are issued by the federal government and a requirement for MC number is that they have commercial insurance. This is for the safety of the other people on the road as well as the driver. They are required to keep log books as well as follow the laws as to how many hours a day they can work.

Because of the huge cost of commercial insurance many transporters bypass this. They also bypass it because of the regulations that makes them have safe equipment and log books. As one might expect it cost money to keep up with truck maintenance and because log books makes it so you can only drive safe and not work to many hours then that cuts down on revenue as well.

Be careful because transporters are permitted to lie on UShip all they want about their status and all of them claim that they are in fact illegal when my quick search of 200 transporters found only 1 that was legal. You can look up any legal transporter in the US simply by the name by going to this site.

http://safer.fmcsa.dot.gov/CompanySnapshot.aspx

Enter in the name or the DOT or the MC number and you will not only get who they are owned by but you will get the current status, insurance company and coverage, inspection reports, accident records but even more importantly you will get the telephone number to contact them directly and save money. This all of course if they are in fact legal and not illegal.

I personally wouldn't piss on an illegal transporter if he was on fire, I have zero respect for them and couldn't care less when they get scraped off the pavement except it slow down traffic and that cuts into my bottom line.

Legal Shipper

A legal transporter is one that takes the time and spends the money to follow the laws. You will know them because they always have the DOT/MC information on the side of their trucks, they will also have to charge more because of the insurance and rules they have to follow.

Some things to remember when using a legal shipper are;

1) The rates are generally more because
   a. Instead of paying $75.00 a month insurance they pay $750.00 and more.
   b. They have to drive by the DOT rules and that means they can only drive or be on duty 14 hours a day.
   c. They have to keep their equipment safe or they get shut down.
   d. Paperwork and overhead are generally time consuming and cost money

You can look up any legal transporter in the US simply by the name by going to this site.

http://safer.fmcsa.dot.gov/CompanySnapshot.aspx

Enter in the name or the DOT or the MC number and you will not only get who they are owned by but you will get the current status, insurance company and coverage, inspection reports, accident records but even more importantly you will get the telephone number to contact them directly and save money. This all of course if they are in fact legal and not illegal.

So if you're a legal transporter then great go out there armed with this resource and maximize your income. Use this knowledge based on my experience and go the extra mile. Be safe and enjoy the country and all it has to offer.

If you're an illegal transporter then try to wreck where it doesn't slow down traffic and stay out of my way as well as out of the way of other legal hard working transporters, we work hard and play by the rules with real drivers licenses, insurance and businesses and unlike you we provide a service that has a value to it.

ABOUT THE AUTHOR

I am Terry, I have 20 + years in technology including VoIP, Networking and Software design. I owned a technology company for 18 years working with large hospitals, government agencies, businesses and the general population. I also own a transportation company.

I generally tell things like they are while using plain language. I feel that if the words have to be steam cleaned and pressed to be on pages then they aren't worth reading.

Enjoy the books and the different style of writing.